Lift Your Head

Amanda Harris

BookLeaf
Publishing

Lift Your Head © 2023 Amanda Harris

All rights reserved.

No part of this publication may be reproduced, stored in a retrieval system, or transmitted, in any form or by any means, electronic, mechanical, photocopying, recording, or otherwise, without the prior written permission of the presenters.

Amanda Harris asserts the moral right to be identified as the author of this work.

Presentation by *BookLeaf Publishing*

Web: www.bookleafpub.com

E-mail: info@bookleafpub.com

ISBN: 9789357748162

First edition 2023

To my babies Gracelynn and Peyton. I want you to see that you can do anything you set your mind to. Don't let any of the negative voices stop you. God has great things in store for each of your lives.

ACKNOWLEDGEMENT

To all of those who have believed in me, thank you!
To all of those who have encouraged me, thank you!
To all who have been a friend when others walked away, thank you!
Each of you holds a special place in my heart and life and I would not be where I am today without you.

Lift Your Head

Sometimes, they will never understand.
So don't try, and don't cry.
God has got you by the hand,
and he has a plan.

So just trust, you must, then let go.
God will take control.
Now you lift your head.

Jesus Is The Way

The waves are crashing
and the sun is fading fast.
Much like the soul within.

A tug-of-war is taking place,
and strength is growing thin.

It's a battle in every way,
but they know they can not sway.
For Jesus is the way.

The Little Children

See the little children?
They are all around.
See the little children?
In them, his love abounds.
See the little children
looking up at you?
See the little children
wondering what he'll do?
See the little children
with eyes shining bright?
See the little children
carrying his light?
See the little children
so full of faith?
See the little children
bow their heads to pray?
See the little children
he's about to use?
See the little children?
Their about to bloom

That Beauty Over There

Can you see her
that beauty over there?
Can you see her
dancing without a care?
Can you see her
that beauty over there?
To stay silent,
She does not dare.
Can you see her
that beauty over there?
She's boldly praying
and devil-slaying.
Can you see her
that beauty over there?
She's not playing
she's not straying

Victory has Come

She has felt the hurt.
She has felt the pain.
She has almost went insane.

She has sat.
She has cried.
She has even tried to hide.

She has run.
She has fought.
The Lord has taught.

Now it's time
to stand and fight.
Fight with all her might.

She has won!
It's done!
Victory has come!

I See You

I see you filled with guilt and shame,
and only yourself you blame.
I see you hiding over there,
just wishing someone would care.
I see your attempt to hold back the tears,
and how you sit with all of your fears.
I see you with all of that pain,
and wonder how you're still sane.
I see you fight that fight.
The load you carry is not light.
I see you start to break.
You wonder how long it will take.

Lord Help Me

Lord help me I'm calling,
for only you can see me falling.
Lord help me to stand and fight,
for Lord, I need your sight.
Lord help me to find my way,
for without you, I would stray.
Lord help me to grow,
with only the wisdom you bestow.
Lord help me shine your light.
Lord, can you make it bright?
Lord help me to love like you.
Then the lost we can pursue.

Preacher Boy

Preacher Boy, Preacher Boy
That's who I'm gonna be.
Preacher Boy Preacher Boy
only if God calls me.

Worship gets my energy,
and I pray every day.
Jesus is my savior.
For him I am bold.

I run.
I shout.
I dance about.
In him, I have no doubt.

Preacher Boy, Preacher Boy
That's who I'm gonna be.
Preacher Boy, Preacher Boy
Only if God calls me.

I'm Sorry I Can't

I'm so sorry,
but I can't go there.
God's approval means the most.
Without him I'd be toast.

I'm so sorry,
but I can't do that.
I know to you it's unfair,
but to disobey God, I would not dare.

I'm so sorry,
but I can't say that.
To you it may sound cool,
but for me I'd be a fool.

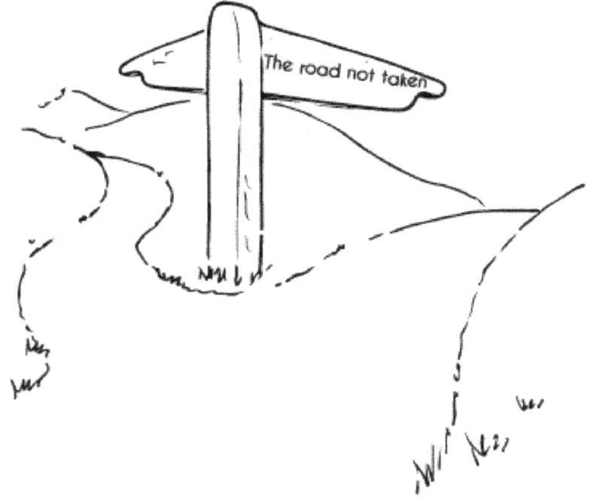

With Jesus

For only his will do I care.
To disobey him I do not dare.
He holds my life in his hand.
For without him, I could not stand.
For without him, I'd be a sinner.
But with him I'm a winner.
Because of him my cup is full.
But Satan's plan is to lull.
Satan is the master of deceit.
Jesus Christ I must entreat.
To live for him we can't be shy.
For in eternity we will cry.

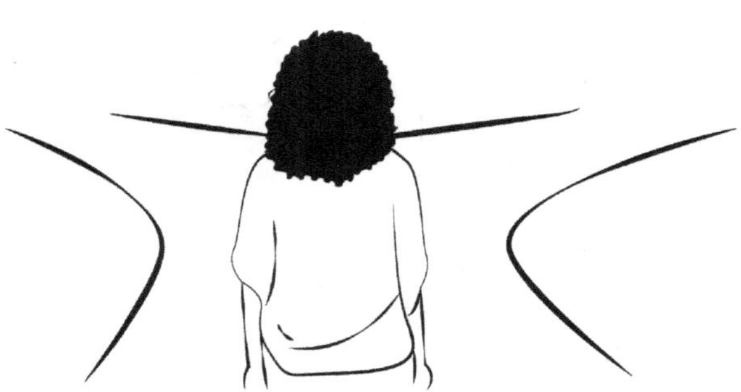

She is a Runner

She's a runner,
from the hurt,
from the pain,
and from anything new.
She's a runner,
from the unknown,
from her failures,
and from her fears.
She's a runner,
from confrontations,
from rejection,
and from hard conversations.
She's a runner and it's all she has ever known.

A Time

They stand in the shadows
waiting to be known.
They stand in the shadows
waiting for hope.
They stand in the shadows
cheering others on.
They stand in the shadows
waiting to be told.....

It's your time!
A time for love.
A time for laughter
of pure joy thereafter.
A time of growth.
A time to win.
A time for life to begin.

Jesus I Need Your Attention

Jesus, I need your attention,
There are a few things, I'd like to mention.
You have always known me,
even before I heard your name mentioned.
You knew that I would fail.
You knew that I would doubt you,
and even wonder if you existed.
You knew I'd not be perfect,
but you still chose to die.
Jesus, I guess I'm wondering why?

My child, My child,
right now you may not see,
exactly who you will be.
My child, My child,
I have great plans for you.
Just trust me and believe.

Jesus, wait, I need your attention.
I have something else to mention.
How come it's me you chose?
I'm nothing special and everyone knows.
I'm nothing compared to them.
They have talent and the friends.
They have a heritage,

and they are multi-generational.
I know nothing of my family line.
Why am I considered special?
Jesus, I guess I'm wondering why.

My Child, My Child,
right now you may not see,
who you are called to be.
The plans I have for you
are so big and so great.
Just trust me and believe.

Fighter Inside

Don't mess with me,
I'm a fighter inside.
Don't mess with me,
or you're in for a surprise.

Satan came a knocking,
He thought I was weak.
Satan came a knocking,
but he was in for defeat.

Don't mess with me
I'm a fighter inside.
Don't mess with me
or you're in for a surprise.

The Devil came a knocking,
but he was in for a ride.
Devil came a knocking,
but God was on my side.

Don't mess with me,
I'm a fighter inside.
Don't mess with me
or you're in for a surprise.

On a Cross

You hung on a cross.
You took my shame.
You hung on a cross,
and I'm to blame.

You hung on a cross
broken and bruised.
You hung on a cross,
You were accused.

You hung on a cross,
and my past was erased.
You hung on a cross,
as you took my place.

You took my sin,
and made me new.
You took my sin,
and I'll live for you.

In between

Flowers bloom
and flowers fade.
Sometimes they dance along the way.

The sun will rise.
The sun will set.
On that you can bet.

Life begins
and life will end.
It's time to celebrate the joy within.

Pastor

Our pastor
He carries a burden like no other knows.
He carries the weight of our soul.
He prays for us when we are ill.
Then when we slip even still.
He fights many fights because he is to lead.
He fights the fights we can not see
It's not just him, but his family.

Sin

Sin is Sin,
there is no way for you to win
There is no little.
There is no big.
Sin is Sin,
and that's the end.

Battles

When a battle comes
act with Wisdom.
When a battle comes,
don't act with emotion.
When a battle comes,
it's best to turn to Him in prayer.
When a battle comes
it's time to stand your ground.
Don't waver and don't fear.
God has got you my dear.

www.ingramcontent.com/pod-product-compliance
Lightning Source LLC
Chambersburg PA
CBHW070734160726
48003CB00006BA/2513